Supernatural Invasion

Supernatural Invasion
Heaven's License
for an Earthly Interference

Dr. C.A. Turner

LITTLE ROCK, ARKANSAS

Supernatural Invasion
Copyright © 2021 by Carlos Turner

All rights reserved. No part of this book may be photocopied, reproduced, distributed, uploaded, or transmitted in any form or by any means, or stored in a database or retrieval system, without the prior written permission of the publisher.

J. Kenkade Publishing
6104 Forbing Rd
Little Rock, AR 72209
www.jkenkadepublishing.com
Facebook.com/jkenkadepublishing

J. Kenkade Publishing is a registered trademark.

Printed in the United States of America
ISBN 978-1-955186-10-0

Unless otherwise noted, scripture quotations are taken from the King James Version® Bible, Public Domain. Used by permission. All rights reserved.

The views expressed in this book are those of the author and do not necessarily reflect the views of Publisher.

Table of Contents

Introduction..7
Chapter 1: Alignment for Access..........................13
Chapter 2: Prayer- The First Key............................23
Chapter 3: Fasting- The Power Key........................35
Chapter 4: Watching- The Master Key..................47
Chapter 5: Living Supernaturally............................61
Conclusion...71
About the Author 73
About J. Kenkade Publishing 75

Introduction

One day, I was meditating on the Word when I saw an open vision. I saw a circle with a watch in it. What was strange about the watch was that it was rolling, and I saw a man running behind it, chasing the watch. Then, all of a sudden, it hit me in the pit of my belly: many are behind time! There's so much God wants to do in the earthly realm, but men fail to totally surrender to the will of God. The reason why this is important to understand is because everything that the Father wants to do has to be done through Man, and He has given Man dominion in the earth to do what He needs to get done!

And God said, Let us make man in our image, after our likeness: and let them have dominion over the fish of the sea, and over the fowl of the air, and over the cattle, and over all the earth, and over every creeping thing that creepeth upon the earth. So God created man in his own image, in the image of God

created he him; male and female he created he them.
Genesis 1:26-27

This is about to upset many people who read this, but I have been teaching this for years: God is not in control! What? That's right; He has given Man dominion in the earth! So, whatever happens in the earth is not God's fault; it's the actions of Man that invite evil things in the earth with our words and thoughts! God has given the earth to Man to rule over, reign in, and dominate!

The heaven, even the heavens, are the LORD'S: but the earth hath he given to the children of men.
Psalm 115:16

Matter of fact, after giving Adam (Man) dominion, God brought all the animals to Adam to give them names.

And out of the ground the LORD God formed every beast of the field, and every fowl of the air; and brought them unto Adam

to see what he would call them: and whatsoever Adam called every living creature, that was the name thereof. And Adam gave names to all cattle, and to the fowl of the air, and to every beast of the field; but for Adam there was not found an help meet for him.
Genesis 2:19-20

You see, God has given us the dominion, power, and authority to maintain the flow and function of the earthly realm. It's clear we have allowed the enemy to rob us of that dominion by not staying in alignment with the Word, will, and ways of God! That's why evil has become a stronghold in the earth because it's time for the people of God to take back their rightful place. Hallelujah!

There's getting ready to be a supernatural invasion that will hit the earthly realm in a mighty way. I can sense a spiritual awakening unfolding. The earth shall be filled with the glory of the Lord, and many shall be healed, delivered, and set free!

For the earth shall be filled with the knowledge of the glory of the LORD, as the waters cover the sea.
Habakkuk 2:14

This supernatural invasion is going to shake the earth, and the Bible said the earth shall be filled with the knowledge of His glory. In other words, everybody will know that this is God's doing. Are you ready to access it? Let's get back in alignment for His name's sake!

Rhema Notes

_____
_____
_____
_____
_____
_____
_____
_____
_____
_____
_____

Supernatural Invasion

Carlos Turner

Chapter 1

Alignment for Access

Growing up in Osceola, Arkansas, I can remember us kids wanting to be superheroes. We had heroes like Superman, Batman, and Wonder Woman (for the girls), to name a few. The one thing that all the heroes had in common was they all had an ability to do something above everyone else's natural ability. As kids, the reason why we were drawn to them was because they could do things that others couldn't do, and they would use the ability they had in order to help somebody else and ultimately save the day.

Although my childhood superheroes weren't real, they prepped my mind and fed my faith in a real hero that would help and assist me later in life. His name is Jesus; do you know Him? He is currently my superhero, and He is the greatest example of what walking in the supernatural really looks like. In the first century, seeing and experiencing the supernatural were common, but not so much today.

It seems to me that the body of Christ is too comfortable with no real desire to operate in the things of the supernatural! We have been robbed of our spiritual capacity by focusing on things that are of this world instead of those things that are above or that are of the spirit. It is the will of the Father that we seek those things which are above.

If ye then be risen with Christ, seek those things which are above, where Christ sitteth on the right hand of God. Set your affection on things above, not on things on the earth. For ye are dead, and your life is hid with Christ in God. Colossians 3:1-3

This is the reason why I thank God for Jesus because He came to be our example so we could be and do what He wants! As a matter of fact, He said we would do greater than what He has done.

Verily, verily, I say unto you, He that believe on me, the works that I do shall he do also; and greater works than these shall he do; because I go unto my Father.
John 14:12

But Jesus' desire and focus were on things that were supernatural more than things that were natural.

So, what is Jesus saying in John 14:12? It's perfectly clear! He is saying He's going to be with our Father (God) and if we just believe in Him and His works, we, too, are going to be able to do what He did. What are some of the "works" of Jesus? He opened up blinded eyes, He healed the sick, He performed miracles, He caused the lame to walk, and He raised the dead! So, Jesus– even though He was in a natural body just like us– did supernatural things to bring glory and honor to our Father.

It's safe to say that in John 14:12, Jesus was suggesting to all believers that we shouldn't be limited to just the natural realm because through Him, we have access to the supernatural. But you must seek those things which are supernatural and not love the things that are in the earth, and you will see that there are no limits in your life. I want to prophesy to you that as you read this book, all limitations are coming off in Jesus' name.

I need to make this clear: having the capacity to operate the supernatural is not for you to become some god or someone to be look up to as some great one. It's available so that spiritual gifts and spiritual abilities can be used to bring non-believers back to the Father! Flowing in, with, and through the supernatural will always give you an opportunity and a platform to introduce Jesus and salvation and the love that the Father has for His people!

The door of the supernatural has been locked up for many believers for too long. Now, it's time to unlock it. There's a supernatural invasion that's taking place. It is my prayer for you that you don't get left behind but learn how to access it. How can we access it, you may be asking? God has already given us the keys to the Kingdom.

And I will give unto thee the keys of the kingdom of heaven: and whatsoever thou shalt bind on earth shall be bound in heaven: and whatsoever thou shalt loose on earth shall be loosed in heaven.
Matthew 16:19

As we can see, we have the keys. The problem is we don't know how to use them! Being a professional detailer, I clean all types of vehicles, and about seven years ago, I start noticing that the way certain cars had to be started had changed. It used to be that you could put the key in the ignition to start a car; nowadays, they give you something called a key fob, and all you have to do is have it in your hand and push a button, and the car will start.

Boy, I had problems with it at first because my customers would leave me this small, black remote-like thing in my drop box, then I would call them immediately and ask them where the key was. They would reply, "I left it with you." I was looking everywhere to see how to start the vehicle, and I quickly learned times had changed, and so had keys. There was nothing wrong with the key that I had, even though it looked different; the problem was I didn't know how to use it even though I had access to it.

That's what's going on in the body of Christ. We have the keys, but we don't know how to use them. Even though we have access to the things of the supernatural and the things of the spirit, we don't understand the keys that have been given to us. What does the Word have to say about it?

Wisdom is the principal thing;
therefore get wisdom: and with all thy
getting get understanding.
Proverbs 4:7

In this powerful book, I'm going to teach you about the different keys and how to use them to access the supernatural. Your time is now! Are you ready? Let's go!

Rhema Notes

Carlos Turner

Supernatural Invasion

Carlos Turner

Chapter 2

Prayer- The First Key

Seek you first the kingdom of God amd all these things will be added to you.
Matthew 6:33

If there were ever an area that the enemy fights us the most, it is the area of prayer. The devil hates for us to spend time with God. I was raised in the Church of God in Christ denomination, and we would have a mother always say, "Little prayer, little power, much prayer, much power!" Now, in my years of study and seeking the things of God, I have never seen that in the Bible, but I found that to be very true even in my own personal life. In the life of Jesus, I'm sure the disciples would be wondering what He was doing when He would separate Himself from them for periods of time. You would always read He went somewhere to pray.

And they that did eat of the loaves were about five thousand men. And straightway he constrained his disciples to get into the ship, and to go to the other side before unto Bethsaida, while he sent away the people. And when he had sent them away, he departed into a mountain to pray.
Mark 6: 44-46

Jesus understood that His ability to do anything came from spending time with the Father! We live in a fast-paced world, and the enemy keeps us busy so we can't carve that time out to spend with the Father. Most people pray when they are sick or in trouble but don't understand prayer is a relationship that's established between you and the Father, and it's not a debit card for blessings. Because of this lack of knowledge, many just don't pray, which causes them to miss things they need to know in this Earth experience.

My people are destroyed for lack of knowledge: because thou hast rejected knowledge, I will also reject thee, that thou shalt be no priest to me: seeing thou hast forgotten the law of thy God, I will also forget thy children.
Hosea 4:6

Because many don't see the benefits at the time, many begin to question prayer, not knowing God is ready to help and bless, but He looks at your consistency and commitment, as well.

What is the Almighty, that we should serve him? And what profit should we have, if we pray unto him?
Job 21:15

Let's be honest, have you ever been there? Let's go further: the question that many ask is, "What is prayer?"

Prayer is a divine communication system designed to exchange information between you and the Father! Prayer is time set aside where you share your love, concerns, and desires with the Father, and He shares in return His love, instructions, and directions with you. Now, do you see why the kingdom of darkness would do anything to keep you out of prayer? There's power in prayer! When you spend quality time in prayer, He gives you power to handle anything and everything going on in the earthly realm.

I know you might be asking, "Where does the power come from in prayer?" The power comes from having His love, instructions, and directions! Yes, do you see how can you lose with that combination? When you are praying, you are basically saying, "I trust the Father to love me, instruct me, and direct me." As a matter of fact, He told us to do just that – He told us to trust Him. Let's look into the Word.

Trust in the LORD with all thine heart; and lean not unto thine own understanding. In all thy ways acknowledge him, and he shall direct thy paths. Be not wise in thine own eyes: fear the LORD, and depart from evil.
Proverbs 3: 5-7

The word "trust" come from the Hebrew word "Batach", which means "to have total confidence in and to have security".

That's major because when I go to the Father in prayer, what Solomon was saying was to go to Him with confidence, knowing He is your security. In other words, I can trust Him with the concerns of my heart being protected. So, as my Father, He gives me instructions and directions, but as my God, He is my security team, protecting what I trusted Him with, which is my heart. Wow! What a mighty God we serve!

So, now Hebrews 4:16 make sense. Let's take a look...

Let us therefore come boldly unto the throne of grace, that we may obtain mercy, and find grace to help in time of need.
Hebrews 4:16

I can come bodly. Why? Because I have the confidence and security. Glory to God!

Let's go deeper. It's very important that you find a place to pray. Of course, Jesus spent time praying in the mountains in that day. I know many will say, "You can pray anywhere", and that's true, too, to a certain degree. However, meeting the Father in a certain place shows consistency and commitment. Having a place to pray matters even from the beginning of time.

Let's take a look:

And the LORD God called unto Adam, and said unto him, Where art thou? And he said, I heard thy voice in the garden, and I was afraid, because I was naked; and I hid myself.
Genesis 3:9-10

Most scholars agree that the reason why the Father asks, "Where art thou?"

was because He and Adam had a meeting place in the garden, a place where he spent time with the Father, and when Adam sinned, he didn't meet the Father at that place, which caused the Father to ask, "Where art thou?" Once you establish a place for you and the Father to commune, stick to that place, meet Him there often, and watch what He will do! Jesus gave us some advice on how to do it.

But thou, when thou prayest, enter into thy closet, and when thou hast shut thy door, pray to thy Father which is in secret; and thy Father which seeth in secret shall reward thee openly. But when ye pray, use not vain repetitions, as the heathen do: for they think that they shall be heard for their much speaking. Be not ye therefore like unto them: for your Father knoweth what things ye have need of, before ye ask him.
Matthew 6:6-8

It's safe to say that Jesus was showing us how supernatural power was flowing through Him. He would get away in a secret place, and what was done when nobody was watching gave Him power to perform supernatural miracles, signs, and wonders when everybody was watching.

So, now, the question that remains is, "Is there any reason why the Father won't answer my prayers?" Unanswered prayers stop the flow of the supernatural.

Here are three major reasons why believers' prayers are hindered:

1. Unconfessed Sins

> *If I regard iniquity in my heart,*
> *the Lord will not hear me.*
> *Psalm 66:18*

2. Unbelief

If any of you lack wisdom, let him ask of God, that giveth to all men liberally, and upbraideth not; and it shall be given him. But let him ask in faith, nothing wavering. For he that wavereth is like a wave of the sea driven with the wind and tossed.
James 1:5-6

3. Refusing to Submit to the Word

Because I have called, and ye refused; I have stretched out my hand, and no man regarded; But ye have set at nought all my counsel, and would none of my reproof: I also will laugh at your calamity; I will mock when your fear cometh; When your fear cometh as desolation, and your destruction cometh as a whirlwind; when distress and anguish cometh upon you. Then shall they call upon me, but I will not answer; they shall seek me early,
but they shall not find me.
Proverbs 1:24-28

Prayer is a major key to the supernatural! If we are going unlock the supernatural, prayer must become a life style not just something that we do. In the book of James it teaches us how to get our house in order and what prayer can do with a pure heart.

Confess your faults one to another, and pray one for another, that ye may be healed. The effectual fervent prayer of a righteous man availeth much. James 5:16

Let's make prayer a priority again so we can have the key that gives us the power to operate in the supernatural. Get back in alignment so prayer can thrust you into your rightful place! Remember, prayer is the key, and faith unlocks the door.

Rhema Notes

Supernatural Invasion

Carlos Turner

Chapter 3

Fasting- The Power Key

I was introduced to the power of God at a young age. I can remember being drunk in the spirit at the age of twelve. I remember shutting-in with the old saints as a teenager on Fridays and Saturdays. It would be me and a few other children at the shut-in. There was a woman who introduced me to the master key to operate in the supernatural. As a kid, I would ask a lot of questions because I needed to know how salvation and being filled with the Holy Ghost worked. I would see many lay hands on the sick, and they'd recover. I have witnessed many prophetic words that came to pass within a few days. I know women who would have dreams, and then something would happen the way they dreamt it.

So, one day, after a revival– I will never forget it– I asked evangelist Clara Jones, "What's the secret to be used by God?" She said, with a serious look, "You have to be willing to die." I said, "Die? I'm not ready to die." She said, "You have to die to your flesh." I asked her, "How can you die and still live?" She said, "You have to fast, push your plate back, and use that time to seek the Lord. I was like, "I don't know about that, but I will try."

I went on a three-day fast– just water– and almost died. But I was hungry for God, and after my first fast, I started to see things happen before they happened. After that, to this day, fasting has been a lifestyle, and it definitely is a power key to the supernatural.

Let's find out what fasting is and what the Word has to say about it.

Fasting *is abstaining from food and pleasure in order to seek God for His ways, will, and wisdom.*

To seek His ***ways*** is to know ***how*** to do. To seek His ***will*** is to know ***what*** to do. To seek His ***wisdom*** is to know ***when*** to do it. Now, read that again and get that in your spirit. That's how powerful fasting can be, but it takes discipline and focus.

Jesus started His ministry off with fasting. When you are fasting, you can prepare yourself to be tempted and challenged by the enemy. The devil knows that the key of fasting gives you direct access to supernatural power! Let's take a look in the Word.

Then was Jesus led up of the Spirit into the wilderness to be tempted of the devil. And when he had fasted forty days and forty nights, he was afterward an hungred. And when the tempter came to him, he said, If thou be the Son of God, command that these stones be made bread. But he answered and said, It is written, Man shall not live by bread alone, but by every word that proceedeth out of the mouth of God. Then the devil

taketh him up into the holy city, and setteth him on a pinnacle of the temple, And saith unto him, If thou be the Son of God, cast thyself down: for it is written, He shall give his angels charge concerning thee: and in their hands they shall bear thee up, lest at any time thou dash thy foot against a stone. Jesus said unto him, It is written again, Thou shalt not tempt the Lord thy God. Again, the devil taketh him up into an exceeding high mountain, and sheweth him all the kingdoms of the world, and the glory of them; And saith unto him, All these things will I give thee, if thou wilt fall down and worship me. Then saith Jesus unto him, Get thee hence, Satan: for it is written, Thou shalt worship the Lord thy God, and him only shalt thou serve.
Matthew 4:1-10

As you can see, if the enemy will attack and tempt Jesus, the Son of the living God, who are we? But we have the same power and authority over the devil to put him back in his place. Never give him a place or space!

Neither give place to the devil.
Ephesians 4:27

When fasting, the devil tries to make penetration because you are at a weak point, but James gives us some advice.

Submit yourselves therefore to God.
Resist the devil, and he will flee from you.
James 4:7

The word **"flee"** comes from the Greek word **"Pheugo"**, which means "to escape out of danger". Wow!

So, it's safe to say that submitting to God gives you the power; so much so that the devil feels like his life is in danger and he has to leave you alone! Why? Because I'm so close to God and so much like the Father, the devil doesn't know the difference between me and God. That's so powerful to me!

Okay, let's go deeper.

It's imperative that we understand God's method for fasting so we won't be fasting in vain. Fasting in vain is good for dieting but not for deliverance.

Moreover when ye fast, be not, as the hypocrites, of a sad countenance: for they disfigure their faces, that they may appear unto men to fast. Verily I say unto you, They have their reward. But thou, when thou fastest, anoint thine head, and wash thy face; That thou appear not unto men to fast, but unto thy Father which is in secret: and thy Father, which seeth in secret, shall reward thee openly.
Matthew 6:16-18

So, let's take a look at the four rules for fasting:
1. Don't impress people with an obvious spiritual demeanor to showcase that you're fasting.
2. Anoint your head with oil.
3. Wash your face.
4. Do it in secret.

Jesus said that if you follow these rules, the Father will reward you openly. In other words, the Father will perform in public what you sacrifice for in secret. You may be asking, "What are some of the benefits that fasting has?" Let's look in the Word.

Is it such a fast that I have chosen? a day for a man to afflict his soul? is it to bow down his head as a bulrush, and to spread sackcloth and ashes under him? wilt thou call this a fast, and an acceptable day to the LORD? Is not this the fast that I have chosen? to loose the bands of wickedness, to undo the heavy burdens, and to let the oppressed go free, and that ye break every yoke? Is it not to deal thy bread to the hungry, and that thou bring the poor that are cast out to thy house? when thou seest the naked, that thou cover him; and that thou hide not thyself from thine own flesh? Then shall thy light break forth as the morning, and thine health shall spring forth speedily: and thy righteousness shall go before thee; the glory of the LORD shall be thy rereward. Then shalt thou call, and the LORD shall answer; thou shalt cry, and he shall say, Here I am. If thou take away from the midst of thee the yoke, the putting forth of the finger, and speaking vanity; And if thou draw out thy soul to the hungry, and satisfy the afflicted soul; then shall thy light rise in obscurity, and thy darkness be as the noonday: And the LORD shall guide thee con-

tinually, and satisfy thy soul in drought, and make fat thy bones: and thou shalt be like a watered garden, and like a spring of water, whose waters fail not. And they that shall be of thee shall build the old waste places: thou shalt raise up the foundations of many generations; and thou shalt be called,
The repairer of the breach,
The restorer of paths to dwell in.
Isaiah 58:5-12

As you can see, there are countless benefits that come with fasting. The question I have for you is: are you ready to die so that your spirit man can stay sensitive to the things of God? Let's not kid ourselves, fasting is not easy at all, but when you become desperate for a miracle or a move of God, fasting grants you access.

Why is fasting so powerful, you may ask? It's because fasting is a form of man humbling himself before the mighty hand of God. In life, I have learned that you are either going to humble yourself or be humbled. The choice is yours, but when you humble yourself for some reason, it moves the heart of God!

Let's take a look in the Word:

But he giveth more grace. Wherefore he saith, God resisteth the proud, but giveth grace unto the humble.
James 4:6

Likewise, ye younger, submit yourselves unto the elder. Yea, all of you be subject one to another, and be clothed with humility: for God resisteth the proud, and giveth grace to the humble.
1 Peter 5:5

Now, the word "**grace**" comes from the Greek word "**Charis**", and one of the definitions is *"to be rewarded"*. So, what Peter and James are saying is that humility positions you to be rewarded by the Father! Now, watch this– all rewards are suggested and directed! Humility suggests you for the reward, and then God directs you to the reward. If we ever want to experience breakthroughs, we are going to have to fast and seek the Lord!

But without faith it is impossible to please him: for he that cometh to God must believe that he is, and that he is a rewarder of them that diligently seek him.
Hebrews 11:6

If victory is in you heart, fasting should be on your mind! There's no need to try to have dominion over a demon if you can't get control and take authority over your appetite. When you push the plate back, God is going to push the miracle up. For those of you who have been fasting, stay encouraged and focused because help is on the way.

Rhema Notes

_____
_____
_____
_____
_____
_____
_____
_____
_____

Supernatural Invasion

Carlos Turner

Chapter 4

Watching- The Master Key

I was speaking to an investor who owns a building complex because I was looking for some office space. He said to me, "I've got several." As we began to look at the many spaces that were available, I noticed that he only had one key. This one key opened every door we went into. So, I asked, "What kind of key is that? And how are you opening every door with the same key?" The man chuckled and said, "I don't have time to go through all those keys. This is a master key, and it allows me to have access to every door in my building."

As I was meditating on this next key, I realized that's exactly what this next key is. It's a master key! Watching is a master key because you can't watch if you don't fast and pray– not to mention that it gives you access to all portals, doors, and gates. A watchman has to be able to locate all portals, doors, and gates in the natural to be a watchman. This is also true in the spirit. A watchman understands that all openings are possibilities. You have to always be aware, sensitive, and alert when you are a watchman on the wall.

We have to start watching again– spending time with God in the night hour! I was raised Church of God in Christ, and they didn't call it "watching"; they called it "shutting in". This was when the saints would come to church on Friday nights and pray all night until Saturday mornings. They wouldn't stop until they ran every devil out and shut every demonic portal of the kingdom of darkness in their territory. Glory to God! We are so distracted now by the things of this world, and the enemy knows it because he is stealing, killing, and destroying, and many have accepted it like it was supposed to be this way. God forbid!

The thief cometh not, but for to steal, and to kill, and to destroy: I am come that they might have life, and that they might have it more abundantly.
John 10:10

Let's dig deeper!

But the end of all things is at hand: be ye therefore sober, and watch unto prayer.
1 Peter 4:7

The number one rule to flowing at a <u>high velocity</u> in spiritual things is that you have to be **SOBER!**

We CANNOT be effective in praying and watching if we are intoxicated with natural things and with carnal minds. Why, you may ask?

It's because you are not going to understand or comprehend the things of the spirit!

But the natural man receiveth not the things of the Spirit of God: for they are foolishness unto him: neither can he know them, because they are spiritually discerned.
1 Corinthians 2:14

In the time we are now living in, you cannot afford unnecessary clutter to be in your spirit. Your spirit must be clean and clear so you can be spiritually effective in this world and shut down every function of the kingdom of darkness in your family and territory. Repeat this with me: "Satan, your kingdom is coming down in Jesus' name!"

The question is: what is a watch?

The word "watch" comes from the Greek word *"kou'stodia"*, which is where we get our English word *"custody"* from. It means "to manage, to take custody and control of", which means you have to be spiritually alert, awakened, and ready to exercise spiritual authority when necessary. The truth is that we have to take back custody of the spiritual airways and stop being lazy! We are dealing with a Prince who's waiting to make penetration and destroy your life.

When you are watching, you are fasting, praying, and abstaining from sleep for certain periods of time in the night hour. You become an intercessor, an individual who can stand in the gap for someone else while they are asleep. They enter in and out of different realms, dimensions, and spheres of the spirit without titles and validation.

A watchmen on the wall contends with three spiritual frontrunners of the watch for the kingdom of darkness:

1. **Demonic Imps**– Dumb spirits that can't think for themselves; they have to be told how and what to do.

2. **Demonic Watchers**– Demons that surveil the activity of a person or area to report back.

3. **Demonic Scanners**– These spirits are like copy machines; they copy and download imitations of a person to function in a false anointing to deceive many and gain access into a family, ministry, or city. A watchman has to be able to pick up on that by operating in high-definition discernment.

We are dealing with a Prince who's waiting to make penetration and destroy your life. The Father shared with me that we are shouting over sermons, prophecy, and material things, not realizing that many have lost *custody*/management, which is our first assignment.

When you have **custody**, it affects spheres and portals, and it's recognized by six Kingdoms and six Realms.

6 Kingdoms:
1. Sovereign Kingdom
2. Angelic Kingdom
3. Galactic Kingdom
4. Planetary Kingdom
5. Adamic Kingdom
6. Animal Kingdoms

6 Realms:
1. Realm of Sowing and Reaping
2. Realm of Life and Death
3. Realm of Expectation
4. Realm of Promotion
5. Realm of Imagination
6. Realm of Spiritual Gifts

We must understand and keep in mind that the Prince of the air understands these kingdoms and realms and will do whatever he can to use them against the children of God.

Let's take a look in the Word:

Wherein in time past ye walked according to the course of this world, according to the prince of the power of the air, the spirit that now worketh in the children of disobedience.
Ephesians 2:2

For we wrestle not against flesh and blood, but against principalities, against powers, against the rulers of the darkness of this world, against spiritual wickedness in high places.
Ephesians 6:12

We are in a spiritual war with real, evil demonic forces with order and rank. We don't have time to be playing in our flesh and flirting with the world. Trust and believe that every day of your life, you are fighting with a thief for your life.

Watch therefore: for ye know not what hour your Lord doth come. But know this, that if the goodman of the house had known in what watch the thief would come, he would have watched, and would not have suffered his house to be broken up.
Matthew 24:42-43

Watch this: the word "thief" comes from the Greek word *"Klep'tes"*, which is where we get our English word *"kleptomaniac"*, which means "to be dominated by the desire to take what others have".

While the church is too busy having church (and is asleep spiritually), the devil is stealing.

That's why we need to reposition ourselves, re-sensitized our spirits, and take back custody of the spiritual airways of the night through the master key of watching. Are you ready to assume your rightful place?

Now, it's imperative to understand the times of the watches you are assigned to. The reason why the devil is stealing like he is is because we love sleep too much, and he gets custody and control. He plots while we are sleeping because many don't want to make the sacrifice to watch and pray.

Another parable put he forth unto them, saying, The kingdom of heaven is likened unto a man which sowed good seed in his field: But while men slept, his enemy came and sowed tares among the wheat, and went his way.
Matthew 13:24-25

You can't be an effective watchman on the wall when you love sleep. I'm sure I just made somebody mad, but watching is a sacrifice.

The four watches of the night are in three-hour shifts. Let's take a look at them:

1st (6pm – 9pm)
2nd (9pm – 12am)
3rd (12am – 3am)
4th (3am – 6am)

Each watch has its own power and anointing.

There are three watch categories you may be called to:

- **Appointed WATCH–** When you are awakened by the Father constantly, every night, at the same appointed time. This means you are appointed to this time watch.
- **Assigned WATCH–** When the Father wakes you up occasionally in different watches for specific reasons, it is called an assigned watch.
- **Assembled WATCH–** It is the gathering of like-minded believers who sacrifice with you for somebody else's breakthrough. This is called an assembled watch.

I want you to take a moment and ask yourself which watch category you are called to.

Let's take it further.

Here are four major reasons why you would need to go on a watch:

1. When you need an answer from God concerning your future and next move **(Hab. 2:1-3)**.

2. When you need a breakthrough of blessings **(Gen. 32:24)**.

3. When people is fighting against your purpose and what you have to do **(Neh. 4:8-11)**.

4. When you're in spiritual warfare **(Pro. 6:4-5)**.

Beloved, if you take watching seriously, you are going to experience God in ways you never could've imagined. I'm not telling you something I heard; I'm telling you from experience! When you start to use the combination of praying, fasting, and watching, the mountain you never thought you could move will move because of your humility and sacrifice. I'm excited about your future because, for many of you, God is about to reintroduce Himself back to you.

Carlos Turner

Rhema Notes

Supernatural Invasion

Carlos Turner

Chapter 5

Living Supernaturally

I believe you are reading this book not because you wanted some feel-good story. I believe you are reading this book because you are tired of the same old stuff. You have made up in your mind that religion is not enough and there is more to God than just a praise and worship team, choir, offering, and sermon. Right? Now, I've got good news for you– you are correct. There's so much more to our Christian walk with God! But here's a question for you. Are you willing to pay the price? Living supernaturally will not be a comfortable, free ride. It'ss going to cost you something! Let's look at the Word.

But he that knew not, and did commit things worthy of stripes, shall be beaten with few stripes. For unto whomsoever much is given, of him shall be much required: and to whom men have committed much, of him they will ask the more.
Luke 12:48

The truth is that many want it but don't want to pay the price for it, and then you have those who are lazy and say things like, "It doesn't take all of that." But isn't it strange that the very ones who feel like it doesn't take all of that are the very ones who want those who make the sacrifices to pray for them? Come on, Zion; we must do better! The earth is groaning for the son of God to come forth.

For the earnest expectation of the creature waiteth for the manifestation of the sons of God.
Romans 8:19

For we know that the whole creation groaneth and travaileth in pain together until now.
Romans 8:22

God's creation is waiting for us to step up and set out. They waiting for us to operate and live supernaturally, not allowing people, places, and things to water us down spiritually.

There's something great on the inside of you, and you are not a mistake. You are here on purpose for a purpose! Think about the things you survived from that should have destroyed you. When you live supernaturally, no weapon formed against you shall prosper.

No weapon that is formed against thee shall prosper; and every tongue that shall rise against thee in judgment thou shalt condemn. This is the heritage of the servants of the LORD, and their righteousness is of me, saith the LORD.
Isaiah 54:17

Paul understood this and lived supernaturally. Let look at Paul experience in the word.

And when they were escaped, then they knew that the island was called Melita. And the barbarous people shewed us no little kindness: for they kindled a fire, and received us every one, because of the present rain, and because of the cold. And when Paul had gathered a bundle of sticks, and laid them on the fire, there came a viper out of the heat, and fastened on his hand. And when the barbarians saw the venomous beast hang on his hand, they said among themselves, No doubt this man is a murderer, whom, though he hath escaped the sea, yet vengeance suffereth not to live. And he shook off the beast into the fire, and felt no harm. Howbeit they looked when he should have swollen, or fallen down dead suddenly: but after they had looked a great while, and saw no harm come to him, they changed their minds, and said that he was a god.
Acts 28:1-6

Now, that's what you call living supernaturally! You're connected to God so much that those who put their mouths on you, expecting you to die, change their minds and call you a god! You need to take a praise break right now! Hallelujah!

I have a prophetic word for you, reader. Get ready– many are getting ready to changed their minds about you! Stay committed and connected. The windows of the heavens are currently opening even right now! I decree that supernatural favor will saturate your life and that the blessing of Abraham will be transferred to you in an abundant way! May the power of the blood of Jesus destroy every bloodline curse from your past and reposition you for your future to walk in divine success in Jesus' name. So be it! Amen!

Are you ready? Are you excited? The Father made a promise that He is going to pour out His spirit on all flesh! In other words, a supernatural invasion is about to happen. It was prophesied by the prophet Joel and repeated again in the book of Acts about this experience in the last days.

Let's look in the Word:

And ye shall know that I am in the midst of Israel, and that I am the LORD your God, and none else: and my people shall never be ashamed. And it shall come to pass afterward, that I will pour out my spirit upon all flesh; and your sons and your daughters shall prophesy, your old men shall dream dreams, your young men shall see visions: And also upon the servants and upon the handmaids in those days will I pour out my spirit. And I will shew wonders in the heavens and in the earth, blood, and fire, and pillars of smoke.
Joel 2:27-30

But this is that which was spoken by the prophet Joel; And it shall come to pass in the last days, saith God, I will pour out of my Spirit upon all flesh: and your sons and your daughters shall prophesy, and your young men shall see visions, and your old men shall dream dreams: And on my servants and on my handmaidens I will pour out in those days of my Spirit; and they shall prophesy: And I will shew wonders in heaven above,

and signs in the earth beneath; blood, and fire, and vapour of smoke:
Acts 2:16-19

Prepare yourself for a move of God that will shake the foundation of the earth! There's getting ready to be a revival that the body of Christ has never seen. There will be an abundance of souls getting ready to come back to God from the ends of the earth. Bodies will be healed, and we will see and experience miracles, signs, and wonders.

But as it is written, Eye hath not seen, nor ear heard, neither have entered into the heart of man, the things which God hath prepared for them that love him.
1Corinthians 2:9

God has a plan with you in mind! Let's get in alignment for the outpour because the latter rain is about to be released.

Carlos Turner

Rhema Notes

Supernatural Invasion

Carlos Turner

The Conclusion of the Matter!

What I love about God is he would allow things to happen just to give himself a reason for show up! The father is in relationship building and there is nothing he wont do for his people! Stay hungry and thirsty and prep yourself to be used! Establish a lifestyle of prayer, fasting and watching! He has place everything you need on the inside of you! How do I know? Because 1John 4:4 says, **"Ye are of God, little children, and have overcome them: because greater is he that is in you, than he that is in the world."** The bottom line is its only a matter of time!

As we continue to seek the will of the father, may his hands be upon you and may he guide you into all truth! I bless you my brothers and Sisters! May the lord bless thee, may the lord keep thee, the lord make his face shine upon thee and be gracious to thee, may the lord lift up his countenance upon thee and give thee peace! Shalom and Amen!

About the Author

Apostle C. A. Turner is the prophetic voice for this last hour. He is the Senior Pastor and Founder of Kingdom Nation Ministries and About God's Business World Outreach ministries in Jonesboro, AR and Memphis, TN. He has been preaching and teaching for over 25 years, reaching the lost at all cost and impacting the earth with the things concerning the kingdom of God with miracles, signs, and wonders operating within his ministry. He attended Grambling State University with a focus in Business Administration. He also Attended the School of Exodus studying Theology and Biblical Studies. He is the founder of Y.E.S.S. Young

Entrepreneur Success School for the urban youth with a focus in financial Literacy. Carlos Turner is the owner and CEO of several successful businesses, Kingdom Clean Detailing, Tojoe's Wings and Waffles, Turner and Thomas Real Estate, Carlo Avery Fashions, and Olive Tree Finance and Investment Firm. In his spare time, he loves reading, studying, and researching the things of the spirit to stay sharp and alert for the things to come! His favorite verse is found in the book of Luke 1:37 that says, "For with God nothing shall be impossible!" His assignment is to shake and reawaken the body of Christ in the area of the supernatural. He understands that this will be a life journey, so he is totally committed to the things of God and strictly being about God's Business.

Our Motto
"Transforming Life Stories"

Publish Your Book With Us

Our All-Inclusive Self-Publishing Packages
100% Royalties
Professional Proofreading & Editing
Interior Design & Cover Design
Self-Publishing Tutorial & More

For Manuscript Submission or other inquiries:
www.jkenkadepublishing.com
(501) 482-JKEN

Also Available from this Author

ISBN: 978-1-944486-78-5
Visit www.amazon.com
Author: Apostle C. A. Turner

A study on the supernatural realm of Dreams, how God speaks to us in our sleep, and what scripture has to say on this matter.

Also Available from this Author

ISBN: 978-1-944486-83-9
Visit www.amazon.com
Author: Apostle C. A. Turner

There's such a hunger for the things of the spirit and the supernatural. Many have decided to tap into the dark side in order to understand more about the Supernatural and the things of the spirit. One of the reasons for this I believe, is because the church as a whole has lost the desire to see a move of God validated by his power with miracles, signs, and wonders. It's my desire and prayer that this information will activate you in ways you never dreamed as you apply it to your spiritual life.

Also Available from this Author

ISBN: 978-1-944486-91-7
Visit www.amazon.com
Author: Apostle C. A. Turner

Lord, Deliver Me delves into the experience of supernatural deliverance in its many forms. Author Carlos Turner explores the methods that the Lord employs to elicit a believer's spiritual discernment and also provides guidance on how a believer can effectively navigate through the highs and lows of healing and freedom. Whether one's hindrances are physical, mental, emotional, or spiritual, God's intention is for us to harness the dominion He has instilled in us to overcome them.